The Best Cartoons from

Leadership
Journal

Volume 1

Well, I haven't actually <u>died</u> to sin, but I did feel kind of faint once!

The Best Cartoons from Leadership Journal

Volume 1

BROADMAN & HOLMAN PUBLISHERS

Nashville, Tennessee

Published by Broadman & Holman Publishers,
Nashville, Tennessee
Acquisitions & Development Editor: Leonard G. Goss

0-8054-1292-1

Dewey Decimal Classification: 817
Subject Heading: HUMOR

01 02 03 04 05 03 02 01 00 99

"I was going to phone the police, but then I thought, 'No, what they need is a pastoral call.'"

"Thanks for agreeing to see me, especially
since my husband said he'd kill anybody
I talked to about our problems."

"You're right, I've never actually been a pirate,
but I think I can understand the world from
a pirate's point of view."

Pete Potley wonders why the Bentons refuse
to acknowledge their previously confessed
codependency problems, until he realizes he
has been counseling with the Watson file.

"Come in, Mr. Fenster. Tell me about your problems."

"Is the coast clear?"

"Give me a cup of strong black coffee and five minutes, and then send in the first victim."

© 1990 David McGinnis

8

"I heard you were here, Pastor,
but I didn't want to cancel our counseling session."

© 1986 Dan Pegoda

Pastor Brackerman secretly wishes that certain folks would leave analogy-making to the professionals.

"Your sermons are wonderful, except occasionally they're a bit too religious."

© 1996 Dan Pegoda

"And this petition requests changing the term 'sinner' to 'person who is morally challenged.'"

"Pastor, there's a man here who needs your help in getting rid of a vice."

© 1984 Nick Hobart

"It's a tricky theological point.
You say you covet your neighbor's humility?"

© 1999 Dik LaPine

"Mr. Norlander, as your gift assessment placement consultant, I have the task of connecting you with the ministry of the church that you have tested most gifted to perform. After much deliberation, it is my conviction that you'd serve the church best as a pew sitter."

"...and our Men's Quiche Fellowship meets
every Sunday morning at seven.'"

© 1994 Mary Chambers

"I can't stand to listen to anyone else preach.
You reckon that means the Lord is calling
me to the ministry?"

"My counseling time is booked solid for the next two weeks. Sorry. But how 'bout a Life Saver™?"

"When I said, 'I'd like to see both of you at 2:30,'
Harry, I meant you and your *wife*."

"According to my horoscope,
this is a good week to preach against false doctrines."

Study Aids

23

© 1988 Andy Robertson

"And, Father, I ask thee now for a good text
to accompany this fantastic joke."

Rev. Roadcup finally finds a friend
to whom he can bare his soul.

26

© 1990 Dan Pegoda

"Let's see, Pastor Leland has Thursday open—
would you prefer regular or quality time?"

"Certainly I make pastoral calls, Mrs. Wilson.
That's what this is..."

"Thank you for calling Eastside Church.
For service times, press 1. For an appointment
with the pastor, press 2. If you were just driving by
and thought our sanctuary would be a pretty place
to get married, press 3."

© 1991 LEADERSHIP. Art: Rob Suggs

"It's Monty Williams. He wants to know if he can audit your discipleship class on total commitment."

"A man from 'Ripley's Believe It or Not!' wants a picture of someone on fire for the Lord."

32

"I know it's early, Pastor,
but I figured you'd be up praying."

© 1986 Doug Hall

"My wife just left me, I lost my job, I need surgery, and my spirits have hit bottom! Pastor, you've gotta help me. What's the difference between pre-, post-, and amillennialism?"

"Oh, good...you're not busy."

"We don't know what you're doing in here, but we've been waiting five minutes to talk to you about the broken hand dryer in the ladies' room."

"How many laps around the baptistry make a mile?"

"The church library just hasn't turned out
the way we had hoped."

© 1988 Erik Johnson

40

The awkward moment after Deacon Bill (L) uttered something much deeper than Pastor Joe (R) usually comes up with.

"We're trying to break down the distinctions between clergy and laity."

Do you ever wonder what the food is going to be like in Heaven? I wonder if they ever serve deviled eggs? Since we'll probably have wings, maybe they'll give us airline food!

Pastor Larry had been watching too much "Seinfeld."

© 1996 Tim Ayers

Suddenly, in the midst of Pastor Fenster's sermon, there it was: a gray area.

"I'd like to see you love *my* neighbor."

© 1994 Doug Hall

"I've stopped expecting you to make leaps of faith,
but it would be nice to see a hop now and then."

Suddenly, trustee Hank Cary ruined
Pastor's symbolism of the newness of life.

"I realize we should not emphasize the rich over the poor, but it's seldom we have a multi-millionaire visit with us."

"You bet it's a gift, and wait till you see
what he does with Lamentations."

© 1985 Rob Suggs

© 1981 Joe McKeever

53

© 1988 Mary Chambers

"In the twenty years I've been here,
I feel I've come to know most of you pretty well."

It occurs to Rev. Billings in the middle of point #2
that point #3 misses the point entirely.

56

© 1988 Steve Phelps

"I wish he were a little less specific
with his illustrations."

"Your sermon really hit home today, Pastor."

© 1996 Jonny Hawkins

"Great message on patience, Pastor.
I loved the way you illustrated by telling those kids
to sit down and shut up."

In one simple illustration, Pastor Ken wipes out the myths of Santa Claus and the Easter Bunny.

"To respond to the charges: Yes, much of last week's sermon was lifted from Scripture, and no, I don't consider that plagiarism."

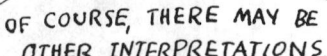

© 1985 Rob Suggs

"Today's message is on the subject of inspiration."

© 1994 Andy Robertson

"I need you to find some choruses to fit in with my message on 'Old Testament Requirements for Cleansing Leprosy on the Scalp.'"

© 1995 Randy Glasbergen

GLASBERGEN

"I'm trying to write a sermon about homosexuality,
but I don't want anyone to know that's what
I'm talking about."

"Tough text, huh?"

Pastor Bergin checks his sources.

© 1998 Steve Phelps

"You know, churches are like parking places: all the good ones are taken, and the only ones left are handicapped."

Why is it that when you need that perfect quote to fit your sermon, the only quote you are able to recall is from a Rolling Stones' lyric?

Why is it that all the big sports events
happen during church?

Pastor Fife reconsiders his innovative
question-and-answer time after the sermon.

"THE BAPTISM"

"Most pastors would've been satisfied
just to *preach* about Jonah and the whale."

© 1985 Doug Hall

"God loves you...but don't let it go to your heads."

© 1992 Rob Suggs

"You're in a rut, Reverend. Every time I come here, you preach about the Resurrection."

© 1983 Doug Hall

"This is my fourth sermon on the transforming power of the gospel. Why do you look like the same old bunch?"

Right in the middle of a righteous rebuke,
Pastor Reggie Coolbaugh blows a finger.

"Pastor takes his visual aids
pretty seriously, doesn't he?"

© 1986 Artemas Cole

"He says there's nothing like
the sound of the King James."

The good people at Oak Ridge Church
had not anticipated
what a sabbatical might do for Pastor Earl.

"Now, a few words concerning the sin of vanity..."

© 1990 Cartoons by Johns

"My sermon today is on humility, and in my opinion it's
one of the finest pieces ever written."

84

© 1994 Jonny Hawkins

"I was going to preach on commitment,
but now I'm not sure."

"I see the pastor is going to preach on
Song of Solomon again!"

"Just kidding...just kidding! I'm not really preaching on
Song of Solomon today."

© 1981 Erik and Vicki Johnson

Johnson

"I'll preach on Thanksgiving, Christmas, New Year's and Easter. You can have 'The Role of Women in the Church,' 'Tongues Speaking for Today,' 'Biblical Inerrancy,' and our special 'Fund Drive Sunday.'"

© 1993 Doug Hall

"Sometimes he skips his regular sermon and wrestles his personal demons instead."

"Pastor Billingsley thought it might be best if
I told you what I told him last night..."

© 1994 Ed Koehler

"Oh, the nursery staff's done gone away,
My intern loves to play,
The budget's nothing but bad news,
The 'lectric organ blew a fuse,
I got them ole deep-down pastorin' blues
Oh yeah...I got them ole pastorin' blues."

"Thanks for agreeing to do the funeral for this friend of
my sister's friend, Pastor. I don't know much about him.
I think he was in some kind of lodge."

© 1983 LEADERSHIP. Concept: Warren Wiersbe. Art: Larry Thomas

"And now the next category—
for the best sermon by a retired minister who uses
the RSV and has never been to the Holy Land."

95

© 1993 Ed Koehler

"We welcome to our pulpit Rev. Windrift,
filling in for our vacationing pastor. The following views
are not necessarily those of the management."

"Powerful sermons, Pastor. Thoughtful, well researched. I can always see myself in them. And I want you to knock it off."

© 1985 Ed Koehler

"Welcome, O weary searcher for truth!
Say, have you ever worked with kids?"

© 1981 Doug Hall

"Okay, 4-year-olds!
Let's polish off the Book of Leviticus!"

© 1990 Andy Robertson

"Okay, kids, these verses memorized by next Sunday or you can kiss your snack time goodbye!"

Armed to the teeth, Sunday school teacher
Nat Willowby prepares to do battle with
the forces of darkness.

© 1997 Doug Hall

"No, Francine. Solomon did not have 300 porcupines."

© 1985 Doug Hall

"As you can see on your handouts,
today's topic is original sin."

"...and on Thursday morning at eleven, our Women Against Evolution, Day Care Centers, Beards, Guitars, and Humorous Messages on the Pastor's Answering Machine will hold their weekly Bible study."

© 1990 David McGinnis

NEW TRENDS IN BIBLE STUDY

The "Turtle Race Method" for selecting a book to study is a real crowd pleaser, despite minor flaws.

"No, Mr. Holmes. We're having an *inductive* Bible study."

© 1980 Larry Thomas

"On second thought, Mr. Smith,
the King James Version may be just right for you."

"Come along quietly, Carl. Your latest birthday puts you with the Middle Agers."

ADULT SUNDAY SCHOOL CLASSES
DIRECTORY

ROOM 102 -- ROMANS
LIGHT ON DOCTRINE, BUT HEAVY ON DONUTS

ROOM 202 -- I JOHN
A CRANKY BUNCH WHO LOVE DOCTRINE AND
DISLIKE DONUTS

LOUNGE -- BASICS OF THE CHRISTIAN FAITH
EXPECT BOB SUNDGREN TO DO MOST OF
THE TALKING

BASEMENT -- POSITIVE PARENTING
BE READY TO TALK SPORTS FOR THE
FIRST HALF HOUR

PORTLOK

Following Pastor Wilkin's sermon on honesty, nothing at First Church remained the same.

© 1984 Doug Hall

"On the other hand, Bozo the Clown has much
to teach us about Christian education."

"Well, I haven't actually *died* to sin,
but I did feel kind of faint once."

"I don't want to be first *or* last.
I want to wallow somewhere in the middle."

You know your Bible study is in trouble when...
The hostess greets you at the door in curlers.

© 1990 Leadership. Concept: David Veerman. Art: Ken Westphal

HOME BIBLE STUDY — 75 A.D.

© 1993 Ed Koehler

"I think Paul wants everyone to say
what this verse means to you."

© 1990 Doug Hall

"No questions, please. I find they disrupt
the flow of my answers."

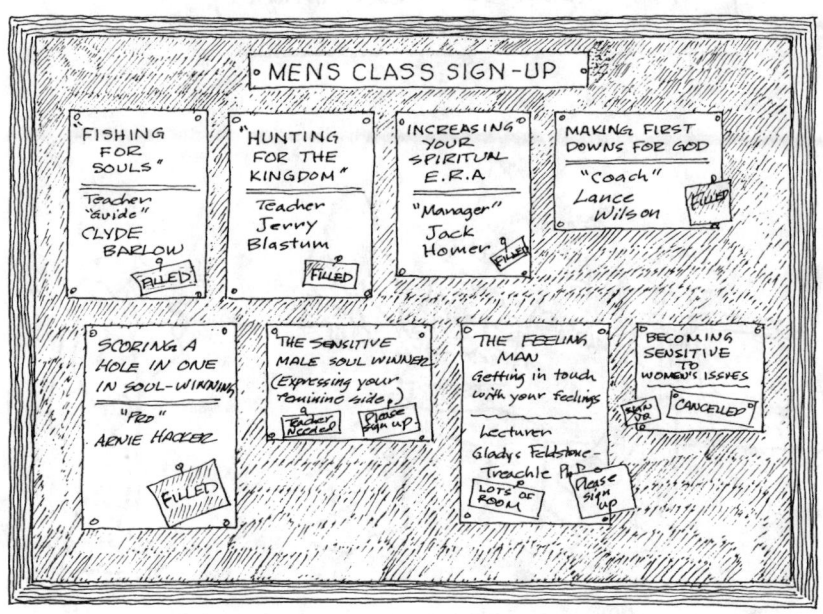

© 1999 Larry Thomas

117

"So far, the only thing we have in common is an aversion to singing, socializing, and sharing."

© 1994 Erik Johnson

© 1992 Doug Hall

"Some churches us the acronym TULIP to remember their beliefs. We use CHRYSANTHEMUM."

ADULT CHILDREN
OF PERFECTLY
NORMAL PARENTS

JOSEPH
FARAS

"And this is our newest support group,
but by far the smallest."

"I, too, was saved from a life of addictions.
I was hooked on phonics."

"Maybe we need to find out more about the groups that rent space from us."

"Tuesday morning...ladies' aerobics."

© 1998 Jonny Hawkins

"Please pray for my husband.
He ruptured himself while venting his spleen."

"I didn't really think we'd get this sign up."

"ACTS OF GOD" as defined by...

THE OAKDALE INSURANCE COMPANY 	Meridian Street Church 	GLADYS THUNDERMUFFIN 
Flood Damage Storm Damage Earthquake Damage Freak Accidents Unforseeable Disaster	The Incarnation Earth You Inspiration Grace Healing Comfort Challenge	LEONARD BUSKIN'S DEVIATED SEPTUM (PUNISHMENT FOR FRIVOLITY) THE HIGGINS' BOY'S "D" IN CHEMISTRY (PUNISHMENT FOR THROWING MY NEWSPAPER INTO THE BUSHES <u>TWICE</u> LAST YEAR)

HALL

"By the time my out-patient surgery got to the end of the prayer chain, I'd had all my limbs amputated, died, and left $100,000 to the building fund."

© 1991 Doug Hall

"Lord, I lay before you the prayer concerns voiced this morning...even though most of 'em sound like whining to me."

"Four days? Boy, time sure flies when you're dead!"

"Have you seen my breastplate of
righteousness anywhere?"

131

"This is a letter from Paul. And these are some study guides, maps, and workbooks I've made available on a no-risk, ten-day trial offer."

"Dear Timothy, I'm sending under separate cover extra copies of the spiritual gifts inventory quiz for your church."

© 1981 Schneider

"I don't know what to think—the weather bureau
says snow, my big toe says partly cloudy,
and the Lord says forty days of rain."

"About my loaves and fishes...
could I get a receipt for tax purposes?"

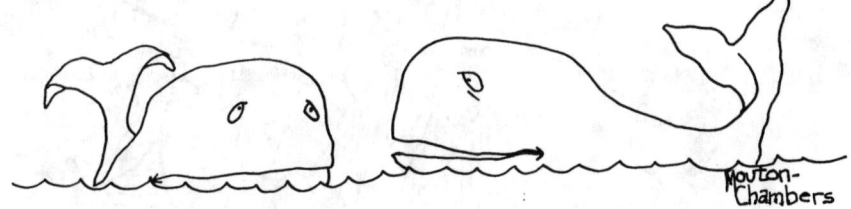

"You wouldn't believe what I had for supper."

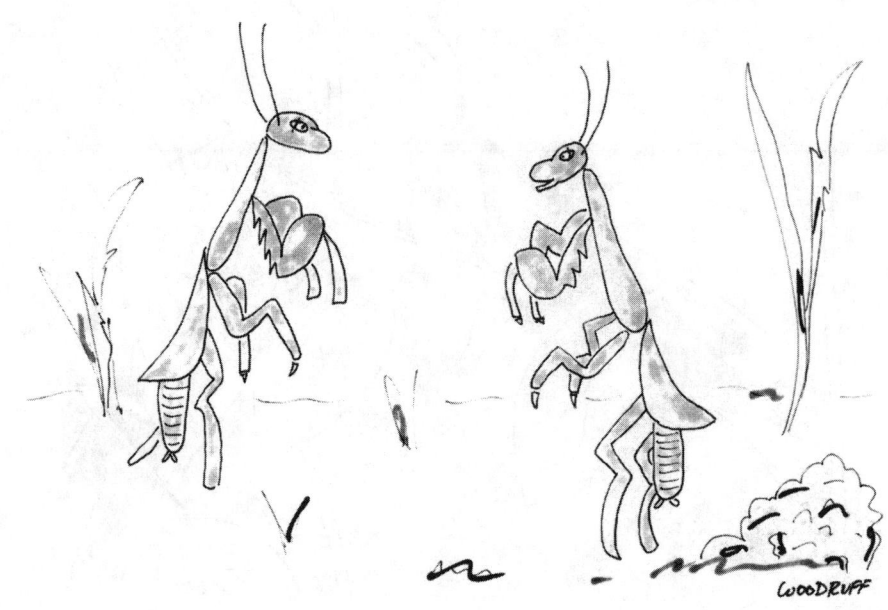

"Sure, everyone thinks we're praying,
but do any of us actually make the time for it?"

© 1981 Goddard Sherman

"I can't help it...I just don't feel like praying."

GOLIATH

PORTLOCK

5:27 P.M.—S.W. Sneedlap remembers he was created just a little lower than the angels.

A Calvinist and an Armenian square off...

© 1997 Mark Sisson

© 1997 Dik LaPine

"Our church's distinctive is to be a *church of grace.*
If anyone can't adhere to that,
we simply ask the person to leave."

"My dear boy, I was practicing self-effacement before you were even thought of."

"Frankly, it does bother me that our
doctrinal statements and church discipline
are issued in a loose-leaf binder!"

"Rev. Jacobs has some peculiar ecumenical theories."

FIRST BAPTIST

TRINITY EPISCOPAL

GENERIC GOSPEL CHURCH

FIRST METHODIST

WESTMINSTER PRESBYTERIAN

© 1993 Ed Koehler

"Maybe we need to define 'community.'"

"Adkins there is pre-trib, Johnson is post-trib, and the fellow with the silly grin on his face stopped studying prophecy years ago."

"Let's sing that old favorite hymn 131...
with each of us altering the third stanza
to suit his or her own views on the Millennium."

152

© 1981 Nick Hobart

"So we're approaching Armageddon.
It's not the end of the world."

"Yes, the signs of the times definitely point
to the end of the world tonight...

"...If you'd like a tape of today's message,
simply write to Box 499..."

"Ten...nine...eight...seven...six..."